Altared Space:
Harnessing Healing Energy Using Feng Shui Principles

Altared Space:
Harnessing Healing Energy Using Feng Shui Principles

Nicholas Cappele

**Altared Space:
Harnessing Healing Energy
Using Feng Shui Principles**

Nicholas Cappele

Copyright © 2012 H2E Design
Phoenix, AZ

All rights reserved. No part of this book may be reproduced or utilized in any form or by any means, electronic or mechanical, including photocopying, recording, or by any other information storage and retrieval system, without the prior written permission of the publisher.

Cover Design by CreateSpace
Photography by Lani Conlkin

ISBN: 0615519067
ISBN-13: 9780615519067

1. Interior design 2. Feng Shui
3. Meditation 4. Self-help 5. Wellness

H2E Design
Phoenix, AZ
www.h2edesignstore.com

Contents

Introduction	ix
FIRST THINGS FIRST	1
Creating Personal Sacred Spaces	3
Introduction to Classic Feng Shui Principles and Tools	5
Calculating Your Personal Gua Number: Men	9
Calculating Your Personal Gua Number: Women	11
The Lo Shu Classic Bagua	12
Understanding the Lo Shu Bagua	13
Yin Yang Theory	15
Wu Xing: The Five Elements Overview	16
Wu Xing: Five Elements Categories	17
Eight Mansions System	28
CREATING YOUR SACRED SPACE	31
Cleansing Your Space	33
Creating an Altar	35
Choosing Sacred Items for Your Altar	37
Altar Items for Gua Aspects of Life (Chart)	38
Dressing Your Altar	39
USING YOUR SACRED SPACE	41
Benefits of Meditation	42
Four Basic Elements of Traditional Meditation	44

Meditation Postures	48
Mantras for Meditation	53
Mala Beads for Use with Mantras in Meditation	57
Introduction to Chakras	59
Root, the First Chakra	61
Sacral, the Second Chakra	63
Solar Plexus, the Third Chakra	65
Heart, the Fourth Chakra	67
Throat, the Fifth Chakra	69
Third Eye, the Sixth Chakra	71
Crown, the Seventh Chakra	73
HEALING THERAPIES	75
Healing with Crystals	77
Healing with Essential Oils	79
Healing with Sound	81
Tuning Fork Sound Therapy	83
Singing Bowls	85
Traditional Singing Bowls	85
Crystal Singing Bowls	87
Gong Sound Therapy	89
In Closing	91
Acknowledgements and Resources	97

Introduction

Being raised a military brat in an Italian Catholic family was my first introduction to the use of the altar as a focal point for spiritual practice. I still have vivid childhood memories of the many churches we visited while we were stationed in Europe. Although I am no longer affiliated with the church, I look back now and realize how much I have been influenced by the rituals of the Catholic mass and by my early exposure to these beautiful ancient churches as I've developed my own spiritual path as an adult.

Later, while struggling to get established in New York City in the 1980s, I was introduced to diverse people from South America, Eastern Europe and Asia. Through exposure to their cultures and beliefs, I learned about their ceremonies, rituals, practices and the creation of sacred spaces centered on altars. At the same time, I was introduced to the philosophy of Buddhism and the ancient art and science of Feng Shui, which opened me to new possibilities and set me on the path of enlightenment that I am still on today.

The world at large can be chaotic and confusing: full of stress, anger, pain and cruelty. Many people are experiencing a desire to go within themselves to find peace, but are at a loss as to how to get started. Creating a sacred space within your home or office can be a powerful first step toward creating serenity and peace in your daily life.

This book will demystify how to create a sacred space within your home by providing a step-by-step approach to setting up a meditation altar using ancient and profound Feng Shui principles of energy. The altar will provide a focus for your meditation practice that will help you harness beneficial energy and create a better life of health, happiness and prosperity.

Thirty years into my spiritual journey, I know that there are many paths to wisdom and it's possible to be overwhelmed trying to decipher them all. This book is designed to provide simple direct information that will enable you to create a beautiful and beneficial space for developing your own path to serenity.

First Things First

First Things First
2 | Altared Space

Creating Personal Sacred Spaces

The Growing Need for Personal Sacred Spaces

For many of us, life is so chaotic and busy that we can lose sight of our true nature and what is really meaningful in our lives. How do we stay connected to a sense of spirit, or to something greater than ourselves? Where can we go to renew, recharge, and restore our relationship with the universe? We may find solace in going to church, spending time in nature, or going on a retreat. But, what about the time in-between?

To address this longing, many of us are looking to create sanctuaries or sacred spaces in our own homes or offices where we can disconnect from the daily grind and reconnect with a sense of the divine. This book is designed to help you create a personal sacred space to relax, unwind, and discover the divine within you.

Deciding Where to Create Your Sacred Space

Depending on the size of your living area, there are many options for setting up your sacred space. If you are fortunate to have a large home, you might set up your space in a spare room or out of the way place that will be undisturbed by daily activity. If you space is small, you might open up a corner, or empty a closet, or even find space on a bookshelf.

No matter what your environment this book will help you put into practice basic Feng Shui principles of energy to create a sacred space that will be uniquely beneficial to you.

The Altar as the Anchor for Your Sacred Space

The focal point of a sacred space is an altar. The altar is the anchor for our energy and the foundation that supports the objects that symbolize our intentions and help connect us to the divine within each one of us. These symbolic objects can include writings, photos, pictures of inspirational figures, saints, sages or loved ones, as well as objects from nature such as rocks, shells, feathers or plants. The specific items we choose to dress our altar will be different for each one of us, and may change with our intentions.

Altared Space will provide an overview of some commonly used sacred objects, and various approaches to dressing your altar in a manner that best matches your own personal spiritual path.

First Things First
4 | Altared Space

Introduction to Classic Feng Shui Principles and Tools

Classic Feng Shui is an ancient art and science developed over 3000 years ago in China. It is a complex body of knowledge that reveals how to balance the energies of any given space to assure the health and good fortune of the inhabitants. The literal translation of Feng Shui means (wind) Feng / (water) Shui. In Chinese culture, wind and water are associated with good health and fortune. Understanding some of the underlying tools and principles of Classic Feng Shui will help you choose the best place to create your sacred space and place your altar to get the most benefit from your meditation practice.

In Classic Feng Shui analysis, the main tools used are the Lo Shu Bagua and the Lo Pan compass. The Lo Shu Bagua is an energy grid containing the symbols of the I Ching, the ancient oracle system on which Feng Shui is based. Knowing the energy centers of the Lo Shu Bagua as they are manifested in your home will help you understand the correlation between these areas of your home and specific areas of your life.

First Things First

6 | Altared Space

Using Your Personal Gua Number to Determine Your Power Directions

There are nine guas within the Lo Shu Bagua that represent the various aspects, elements and energies connected to your life. Based on our sex and our birth date, each of us has our own personal gua number. Your gua number situates you within the Lo Shu Bagua grid, which determines your life group and individual power directions.

Using a Lo Pan Compass to Situate Your Space within the Lo Shu Bagua

In a classic Feng Shui audit, a Lo Pan compass is used to understand the placement of your home, and the Lo Shu Bagua is placed over your floor plan to help you understand the influences of the energy in each of the guas. Once the Lo Shu Bagua is laid on your floor plan it will help guide you in creating an altar space to harness the best possible energy in specific areas you wish to enhance.

Understanding classic Feng Shui energy principles means understanding how the Lo Shu Bagua grid correlates to the directional placement of your home or office and where you "reside" within the grid.

THE LO SHU
CLASSIC BA-GUA

4	9	2
3	5	7
8	1	6

First Things First

How to Calculate a Gua Number for Men

Step one of determining the best possible direction for your altar, is to calculate your personal gua number.

Using the solar calendar and Chinese New Year, Feb. 3-4th, add together the last two digits of the birth year until it reaches a single digit, then subtract that number from 10.

If you reach the number 5, use the number 2 as the Gua number.

If you reach the number zero, take the number 9 as the Gua number.

Example 1: January 15, 1974
In this case, we use the previous year because the birth date is before Feb 3rd. Add 7+3=10. Get a single digit by adding 1+0 = 1, then subtract from 10: 10 – 1 = 9.
In this example, the man's Gua number is a 9.

Example 2: May 1, 1954
Start by adding 5 + 4 = 9
Subtract from 10: 10 – 9 = 1
This man's Gua number is 1.

Please note: If the male child is born during or after the year 2000, subtract from 9

Example 1: A male child is born September 1, 2000
0 + 0 + 0 becomes 9
Subtract from 9: 9 – 9 = 0
The final zero becomes a 9.
This boy's Gua number is 9

Example 2: A male child is born February 1, 2000
Because the birth date is before February 3rd, we take the previous year of 1999
9 + 9 = 18, 1 + 8 = 9
Subtract from 9: 9 – 9 = 0
The final zero becomes a 9.
This boy's Gua number is 9

Example 3: A male child is born April 5, 2002
Add 0 + 2 = 2
Subtract from 9: 9 – 2 = 7
This boy's Gua is a 7.

THE LO SHU
CLASSIC BA-GUA

4	9	2
3	5	7
8	1	6

First Things First
Altared Space

How to Calculate a Gua Number for Women

Using the solar calendar and the Chinese New Year (February 3rd and 4th) add together the last two digits of the birth year until it reaches a single digit. Then add 5 to that number. (It should reach a single digit.)

If you reach the number 5, take the number 8 as the Gua.

If you reach the number 0, take the number 9 as the Gua.*

Example 1: June 21, 1954
Start by adding 5 + 4 = 9, then add 5: 9 + 5 = 14
Reduce to a single digit (1 + 4 = 5)
Female 5's take use 8 as their Gua number.

Example 2: January 18, 1970
Since this birth date is before Feb 4th, use the previous year of 1969.
Begin by adding 6 + 9 = 15.
Before you reduce to a single digit, add 5: 15 + 5 = 20.
Reduce to a single number by adding 2 + 0 = 2.
This woman's Gua number is a 2.

Example 3: November 12, 1961
Start by adding 6 + 1 = 7, then add 5: 7 + 5 = 12
Reduce to a single digit by adding 1 + 2 = 3.
This woman's Gua number is 3.

Please note: if the female child is born during or after the year 2000, add 6.

Example 1: A female child is born on July 12, 2000
Zero becomes a 9*, then add 6: 9 + 6 = 15.
Reduce to a single digit by adding 1 + 5 = 6.
This girl's Gua number is a 6.

Example 2: A female child is born on January 8, 2002
Because she is born before February 3, use the previous year (2001).
Add 0 + 1 = 1, then add 6: 1 + 6 = 7
This girl's Gua number is 7.

Example 3: A female child is born on November 7, 2006
Add 0 + 6 = 6, then add 6: 6 + 6 = 12
Reduce to a single digit by adding 1 + 2 = 3.
This girl's Gua number is 3.

THE LO SHU
CLASSIC BAGUA

4	9	2
XUN (SOON) ELDEST DAUGHTER SOUTH EAST-SMALL WOOD LIVER "The Gentle" Sun symbolizes the wind. As the wind blows in from afar it suggests distance, remoteness & distant places. Wind reaches everywhere hence its attribute of penetration. It also suggests marriage, trade &commerce. It characterizes persevering labor &vehemence. It also suggests purity, completeness, quiet & contemplation, yet also indecision.	**LI THE MIDDLE DAUGHTER** SOUTH-FIRE HEART-EYES "The Clinging" Li is very dynamic, a result of its association with sun & fire, yet it is yin in nature. I traits often include rash behavior, aggressive & an adventurous streak. Arguments are common with Li energy.	**KUN (KOON) THE MOTHER** SOUTHWEST-EARTH STOMACH "The Receptive" represents the mother, the wife & elderly women. Kun has an earthly quality, giving a person such traits as persistence, dependability, and a calm demeanor. They can also be nurturing and supportive.
3 **CHEN (CHUN) THE ELDEST SON** EAST- BIG WOOD LIVER- FEET "The Arousing" Yin in nature Chen symbolizes the launching of energy and movement. It is arousing, the initiator of life. Speed. It represents the east –when the sun rises in the east it brings a sense of vitality and vigor throughout the earth. It is a time of blossoming, expansion the beginning of new things, ventures and new occupations. This is an energy of impatience & surprises in its negative, for it has a strong connotations of robbery.	**5** THE FIVE GUA REPRESENTS THE UNIVERSAL EARTH CENTER	**7** **DUI/TUI (DEWEY)** THE YOUNGEST DAUGHTER WEST- SOFT METAL MOUTH-THROAT-LUNGS "The Joyful" Dui is associated with marshes –low lying places that denote insufficiency, incompleteness, inadequacy, defectiveness & things that are indented or concave. Many strange things can push up from the depths of the lake associations are of reflection, enticement destruction & ruin. Tui means pleasurable and the happy (food drink money) yet danger can result from an excess of pleasure.
8 **GEN/KEN (GUN)** YOUNGEST SON NORTH EAST-MOUNTAIN EARTH BONES-STOMACH "Stillness" because of its association with mountains, Ken has a stubborn and unyielding streak. Its other traits include nobility, dependability, steadfastness and resistance to change.	**1** **KAN THE MIDDLE SON** NORTH-WATER KIDNEYS "The Abysmal" Kan personalities can be moody, anxious and have a strong intuitive and "feeling" nature. They are highly intelligent tending to be scholarly. They tend to have excellent ideas/concepts and are usually very good at making money. Because they are associated with water, they tend to be hard to pin down.	**6** **CHIEN** FATHER NORTHWEST-HARD METAL HEAD "The Creative" associated with heaven and is consequently noble, lofty, and firm. It is light as opposed to dark. It symbolizes the strong, the expansive, and the masculine. it is creative, perpetually moving, never stopping. Opposites confront each other in Chien an it is the time and place for decisive battles to be fought Chien is energy.

First Things First

Understanding the Lo Shu Bagua

The Lo Shu Bagua is divided into 9 quadrants or "Gua," (also called "palaces"), which contain:

The Ming Gua Lo Shu Number (your personal Gua number)
- The Chinese Trigram/Member of the Family
- The location of the Gua on the grid (your power direction)
- The element the Gua represents
- The parts of the body it governs
- The personality attributes and traits

The Ming Gua Lo Shu Number
Your Ming (personal or birth) Gua (trigram) is the guardian star (or number) you were born under. Considering your gender and the year you were born in, you are assigned a number from 1-9 (excluding the number 5) that is affiliated with a five–phase element and a trigram.

Trigrams/Members of the Family
The Lo Shu Bagua contains the eight trigrams, which are balanced equally within the Lo Shu Bagua. The trigrams represent the Mother, Father, Eldest Daughter, Eldest Son, Middle Daughter, Middle Son, Youngest Daughter, and Youngest Son. The center Gua represents the Earth/Center and is neutral.

Aside from gender identity, the trigrams are also associated with many natural & human phenomena: the seasons, magnetic directions, the five elemental phases and their corresponding colors, animals, human personality types, body parts, related illnesses and numbers.

Power Directions/Elements - Each of the Gua are represented with a power direction and a phase element. Example: Gua 1 represents the water element and is found in the north, whereas Gua 9 represents the fire element found in the south direction.

Parts of the Body - Additionally, all of the Guas rule different parts of the body. This information is especially helpful when looking at the strengths and weaknesses in one's own Gua.

Personality Attributes and Traits - Each Gua has a list of personality attributes and traits, such as steadfastness, creativity, dependability, and so on.

Now that you know your individual Gua number and can place yourself within the Lo Shu Bagua energy grid, we can dig a little deeper to understand more about how classic Feng Shui theories of energy can help you create your optimum sacred space.

First Things First

YIN YANG THEORY

Before we go further in exploring the Lo Shu Bagua, it's important to understand the basic underlying concept on which Feng Shui is built, the Yin Yang Theory. The Yin Yang symbol represents the ancient Chinese understanding of how things work. The outer circle represents "everything," while the black and white shapes within the circle represent the interaction of the two energies, called "Yin" (black) and "Yang" (white), which cause everything to happen.

"Yin" represents the feminine energy and is characterized as dark, passive, downward, cold, contracting energy. The "Yang" represents male energy and is characterized as bright, active, upward, hot and expansive energy. The concept of Yin/Yang is the most fundamental and profound theory of Feng Shui; it embodies the Chinese perspective of balance and continual change.

Yin Yang Are Opposites

Everything has its opposite. No one thing is completely yin or yang. Each contains the seed of its opposite. Example: cold can turn into hot, what goes up must come down.

Yin and Yang Are Interdependent

One cannot exist without the other. Example: day cannot exist without night.

Yin and Yang Both Consume and Support Each Other

Yin and yang are held in balance – as one increases, the other decreases and imbalances can occur, such as excess Yin, excess Yang, Yin deficiency, and Yang deficiency.

Yin and Yang Can Transform Into One Another

Energy is always moving and balance is not static. At a particular stage, yin transforms into yang and vice versa. Example: night turns into day, warmth cools; life changes into death.

Part of Yin is in Yang and Part of Yang is in Yin

The dots in each serve as a reminder that there are always traces of one in the other. Example: there is always light within the dark (the stars at night), These qualities are never completely one or the other.

Altared Space | 15

WOOD FEEDS FIRE
FIRE FEEDS EARTH
EARTH CREATES METAL
METAL CREATES WATER
WATER FEEDS WOOD

Wu Xing Five Element Productive Cycle

Wu Xing (pronounced woo zing) means the five transformations of energy or the five phases. All matter or energy can be classified in one of the five elements of Fire, Earth, Metal, Water, and Wood. The ancient Chinese believed that the interaction of the five elements is used to enhance positive chi and correct negative chi to create balance in your space.

I use these principles extensively in my interior design practice to create flow and harmony throughout the client's home or office. These principles are also important to consider when creating sacred space and dressing the Altar.

Each phase element is associated with characteristics, seasons, shapes, colors, directions, numbers, and body parts.

First Things First
18 | Altared Space

Wood (Grows)

CHARACTERISTICS: Kindness, flexible
SEASON: SPRING
SHAPE: Beam-like, grows upward, rectangular
COLORS: Green
DIRECTION: East, southeast
NUMERICAL REPRESENTATION: 3, 4
BODY PARTS: Feet, Legs, Liver, Lower back

First Things First
20 | Altared Space

Fire (Radiates)

CHARACTERISTICS: Vibrant, Hot, the Talker
SEASON: Summer
SHAPE: Triangular, pointed
COLORS: Red, Pink, Orange, and Purple
DIRECTION: South
NUMERICAL REPRESENTATION: 9
BODY PARTS: Heart, Eyes

Earth (Compacts)

CHARACTERISTICS: Stable, trustworthy, stubborn
SEASON: Late Summer
SHAPE: Square or cubic
COLORS: Yellow, Brown, Beige
DIRECTION: Northeast, Southwest
NUMERICAL REPRESENTATION: 2, 8
BODY PARTS: Stomach, Fingers, Hands

Metal (Contracts)

CHARACTERISTICS: Sharp, righteous, loner
SEASON: Autumn
SHAPE: Round Spherical
COLORS: White, Gold and Silver
DIRECTION: Northwest, West
NUMERICAL REPRESENTATION: 6, 7
BODY PARTS: Head, Lungs, Mouth, Chest

WATER (falls)

CHARACTERISTICS: Full of wisdom, liberal
SEASON: Winter
SHAPE: Wavy
COLORS: Blue, Gray, Black
DIRECTION: North
NUMERAL REPRESENTATION: 1
BODY PARTS: Kidneys, Blood, Ears

Eight Mansions (PA CHAI/BA ZHAI) System: Life Gua Number Chart

GROUPS	EAST LIFE GROUP				WEST LIFE GROUP			
CHINESE TRIAGRAMS	Chen	Xun	Kan	Li	Chien	Kun	Gen	Dui
GUA NUMBERS	3	4	1	9	6	2	8	7
SHENG CHI GOOD DIRECTIONS								
+90 BEST FOR MONEY	S	N	SE	E	W	NE	SW	NW
+80 BEST FOR HEALTH	N	S	E	SE	NE	W	NW	SW
+70 RELATIONSHIPS	SE	E	S	N	SW	NW	W	NE
+60 STABILITY	E	SE	N	S	W	SW	NE	W
SHA CHI BAD DIRECTIONS								
-60 NOTHING GOES SMOOTH	SW	NW	W	NE	SE	E	S	N
-70 LAWSUITS, BAD ROMANCE	NW	SW	NE	W	E	SE	N	S
-80 BAD HEALTH, BETRAYALS	NE	W	NW	SW	N	S	E	SE
-90 DIVORCE, FAILURES	W	NE	SW	NW	S	N	SE	E

First Things First

The Eight Mansions system dates back to the Tang Dynasty (960-1279). Within the Eight Mansions system is what's known as the Life Gua and the House Gua methods. The aims of these methods are to combine the best sectors of the house with the individual's best direction (based on their personal Gua number). Your personal Gua places you into either the East or West Life Group. Each group has corresponding positive and negative directions. These are further broken down into Sheng Chi (positive energy) or Sha Chi (negative energy). Knowing your Life Group and corresponding positive and negative numbers will help you determine the best possible direction to set up your sacred space.*

*To fully understand the implications of the +SHENG and - SHA chi that flow through your space I would highly recommend having a Feng Shui consultant do a full audit on your home or office using a compass.

Creating Your Sacred Space
30 | Altared Space

Creating Your Sacred Space

Cleansing Your Space

After you've chosen the location for your personal sacred space and determined the best direction for your Altar based on your personal Gua number, the next step is to undertake a space cleansing ceremony to clear any negative energy in the room. The cleansing ceremony is the beginning of setting your intentions to use this space in a different way than you use other parts of your home. By cleansing the area, you clear out negative energy and set the space apart.

There are a variety of cleansing ceremonies to consider. I always do a walk through with my clients to identify unnecessary clutter (which is a magnet to negative energy). A simple way to change the vibration of the space is through color, with a fresh coat of paint. Once the physical alterations are complete, I would start with a smudging ceremony to remove any residue of negative energy, followed by an orange peel blessing to balance, protect, and bless your space before performing your first ceremony at your Altar.

Smudging

Smudging is a powerful cleansing technique from the Native American traditions with "smudging" being the common name given to the burning of sacred grasses. The three plants most used are sage, cedar and sweet grass. The theory behind the ritual is that the smoke attaches itself to the negative energy present in the space and as the smoke clears it takes the negative energy with it releasing it to the ethers to be regenerated into positive energy.

Orange Peel Blessing

The orange peel blessing is performed on the interior of a house or commercial building and only works on the building itself and the lives of the people who reside within. The freshening power of citrus and water along with Mantras (spiritual sounds) and visualizations refresh the energies of the building and occupants. This ceremony helps create new beginnings and fresh starts in life in the most unfortunate circumstances. Performing this cure is appropriate to bless a home or office upon moving in or to ensure an auspicious grand opening to a new business.

To learn more, contact a local Feng Shui consultant to help explain some of the ceremonies and get you started in the right direction.

Creating Your Sacred Space

Choosing Your Altar

The Altar is the anchor for a sacred space. Altars can be in many shapes, sizes and made of various materials. They can be made on a table, shelf, or even a small nightstand. Some people might want to have more than one Altar inside their home, or additional Altars in their yard or garden. It is important to keep in mind that an Altar should always be at a comfortable level for viewing, whether you are sitting on the floor or seated in a special chair.

Altars are sacred space to house the energy used in your meditation practice. An Altar is a place of power, a place to center your self, a place to harness energy. When you create your Altar, it is important to find something that speaks to you; it is very personal and should reflect who you are. When looking at your Altar you should feel in tune with the spirit.

Altars are a powerful center of energy for ceremony and ritual, whether for individuals using their home altars for meditation, or for congregations gathered together in traditional ceremonies. Every encounter with an Altar can be a two-way flow of spirit between the individual and his or her experience with the divine. As we sit before our own personal Altars we enter into a relationship where the most powerful aspects of ourselves are revealed, where we gain greater understanding of our place in the universe.

When we decide to create our own personal Altar, we are essentially making a commitment to bring our spiritual search home, and in doing so, we ground our journey in the mundane aspects of our everyday life. Our personal altar provides a positive daily affirmation of our spiritual quest.

Creating Your Sacred Space
36 | Altared Space

Choosing Sacred Items For Your Altar

Altars, and the items we use to dress them, are as unique as the individual and there is a certain mystery in what each of us finds to be significant and appropriate. Listed below are some suggested items that are typically used for meditation purposes.

Deity of choice/ photographs of mentors, or loved ones
Candles
Incense
Mala beads
Essential oils
Fresh flowers
Bowl of fresh water
Sacred items storage box
Singing bowls, standing chime/gong, tuning forks
Music CD for meditation
Comfortable clothing

ALTAR ITEMS FOR GUA ASPECTS OF LIFE

WEALTH & ABUNDANCE ELEMENT: WIND COLORS: RED & GOLD ITEMS: DIETIES: LAKSHMI HINDU GODESS OF ABUNDANCE /GANESH(REMOVER OF OBSTACLES) HEALTY PLANT /FRESH FLOWERS SMALL WATER FOUNTAIN SMALL MIRROR TO PLACE IN BACK OF WATER OR PLANT ELEMENT TO DOUBLE PROSPERITY RED & GOLD ITEMS, IMAGERY OF ABUNDANCE, DREAM HOMES, MONEY DREAM CARS ECT. POWER WORDS SUCH AS: "ABUNDANCE","SUCCESS", "WEALTH",	FAME & FORTUNE ELEMENT:FIRE COLOR: RED ITEMS: DEITY:LAKSHMI (GODESS OF ABUNDANCE) TALL HEALTY PLANTS /FRESH FLOWERS RED, ORANGE, YELLOW ITEMS OBJECTS OF RECONITION: TROPHIES, DIPLOMAS, AND CERTIFICATES OF APPRECIATION. RED CANDLES, PICTURES OF PEOPLE YOU ADMIRE WHO YOU WISH TO BE IDENIFIED WITH. A PICTURE OF A TV OR RADIO TO SYMBOLIZE YOUR FAME BEING BROADCAST AROUND THE GLOBE. POWER WORDS LIKE "LEADER","RESPECT" "SUCESSFUL" "INTERNATIONALLY KNOWN"	LOVE & RELATIONSHIPS ELEMENT: EARTH COLORS: PINK PEACH WHITE ITEMS: DEITIES: PAVARTI/KRISHNA/VIRGIN MARY HEALTHY PLANT/FRESH FLOWERS PAIRS OF OBJECTS: TWO CANDLES PICTURES OF TWO PEOPLE PAIR OF LOVE BIRDS ROSE QUARTZ CRYSTAL SMALL MIRROR BEHIND PLANT OR FLOWERS TO MULTIPLY LOVE ENERGY SENSUAL LITERAATURE OR LOVE POEMS HAND WRITTEN WORDS OF POWER: "PASSION","UNCONDITIONAL LOVE" "OPEN HEART","ROMANCE", "I RECEIVE EASILY".
FAMILY ELEMENT: THUNDER COLORS: GREEN ITEMS: DIETIES: VIRGIN MARY/ JESUS/ LEI GONG (GOD OF THUNDER) HEALTHY PLANT/ FRESH FLOWERS WOOD OBJECTS,PHOTOS OF FAMILY & FRIENDS IN WOODEN FRAMES,MEMENTOS FROM LOVED ONES.POWER WORDS SUCH AS "FORGIVNESS", "LOVE", "HONESTY" & "COMMUNICATION".	HEALTH ELEMENTS: EARTH & SUN COLORS;YELLOW ITEMS: DEITIES: MEDICINE BUDDAH/GANESH/ JESUS FRUIT IN A COLORFUL BOWL HEALTHY PLANT/ FRESH FLOWERS SYMBOLS & ITEMS FROM THE EARTH: STONES, SHELLS ,TERRA COTTA POTTERY PICTURES OF THE EARTH, SUNRISE, DAISIES SUNFLOWERS, PEOPLE WHO REPRESENT HEALTH & BALANCE TO YOU A HAND WRITTEN NOTE WITH POWER WORDS SUCH AS "HEALTH"," HAPPINESS" "HARMONY"	CREATIVITY / CHILDREN ELEMENT: LAKE COLORS: WHITE & PASTELS ITEMS: DEITIES: SARASWATI(HINDU GODESS OF CREATIVITY& KNOWLEDGE)/ VIRGIN MARY HEALTY PLANTS /FRESH FLOWERS PICTURE FRAMES MADE OF METAL,STUFFED TOYS,PHOTOS OF CREATIVE GENIUSES PICASSO, MOSART ECT.BABY ITEMSTO ENCOURAGE PREGNANCYYOUR CHILDRENS ART WORK DRAWINGS ADD POWER WORDS LIKE "CREATIVE","INSPIRATION", "CHILDLIKE', "FERTILITY'.
SPIRITUALITY & KNOWLEDGE ELEMENT: MOUNTAIN COLOR: BLUE ITEMS: DIETIES: JESUS/ BUDDAH/ SHIVA/ KRISHNA HEALTHY PLANT /FRESH FLOWERS DEEP BLUE & GREEN ITEMS: BOOKS VIDEOS YOU ARE OR WISH TO STUDY,PHOTOS OF SPIRITUAL MENTORS, MOTIVATIONAL SPEAKERS YOU ADMIRE POWER WORDS SUCH AS: "ENLIGHTMENT" MENTAL CLARITY" "INNER GUDIANCE"	CAREER ELEMENT: WATER COLORS: BLACK & BLUE ITEMS: DEITY; OF GANESH(REMOVER OF OBSTACLES)HEALTHY PLANT/SMALL WATER FOUNTAIN / FRESH FLOWERS MIRROR BEHIND PLANT OR WATER TO DOUBLE ENERGY,EXAMPLES OF YOUR PRESENT OR FUTURE CAREER..(YOUR FAVORITE BOOK IF YOU WANT TO BE PUBLISHED)SYMBOLS OF THE GROUPS ORGANIZANTIONS YOU WANT TO BE AFFILIATED WITH.POWER WORDS SUCH AS "MOTIVATION", "SUCCESS", "PASSION" "CONFIDENCE","CREATIVITY"	HELPFUL PEOPLE ELEMENT: HEAVEN COLORS: GRAY, SILVER, BLACK, & WHITE ITEMS: DIETIES: PAVARATI (THE MOTHER GODESS), BUDDAH/JESUS. HEALTY PLANTS/ FRESH FLOWERS,SMALL FOUNTAIN PICTURES OF ANGELS, SAINTS, SPIRITUAL TEACHERS.THE NAME OF THE PERSON YOU WANT HELP FROM. SYMBOLS OR PICTURES OF COMPANIES YOU WANT TO WORK FOR MENTORS TO COACH YOU A SPECIAL BOX TO HOLD REQUESTS.POWER WORDS LIKE: "GRATITUDE",GUIDENCE", "SYNCHRONICITY"

Creating Your Sacred Space

Dressing Your Altar

Once you have determined the best direction for your Altar and have cleansed the space, it's time to set your intention or focus for your meditation practice. An Altar can be dedicated to nurturing whatever your heart desires. For example, you may want to focus on health issues, relationships, money, or general well-being.

Many of my clients who are familiar with Western Feng Shui terminology often ask if its alright to dedicate their sacred space to the life aspirations found in the western bagua Although I don't use the aspiration chart in my Classic Feng shui practice, I've included a Western Bagua chart only for inspirational purposes in creating your sacred space with intent.

The first consideration in dressing the Altar will be to create harmony and balance through the use of the five elements of Wood, Fire, Earth, Metal, and Water. This can be done through the items placed on the Altar.

Example: The table could be made of Metal, a plant could represent Wood, a clear bowl with fresh cut flowers in the colors dedicated to the gua could represent Water, a terra cotta/ceramic offering bowl or stones could represent Earth, and, of course, a candle would represent the Fire element.

In the following chart I have shown the Western bagua chart. I have listed the aspirations, the element and colors associated with each Gua. Also listed are some ideas, suggestions, and recipes to help you dress the Altar to create balance and encourage energy to fuel your intentions.

Remember these are only suggestions, so to listen to your heart when creating your sacred space. Let your intuition guide you, as nothing is set in stone. If you should wake up one morning and the Altar no longer resonates with you, it may be time to refocus your intentions. Meditate and see what speaks to you. Using the five elements as a guide, select items that will bring you joy in creating a balanced energy to your new intention.

Using Your Sacred Space

Using Your Sacred Space

The Benefits of Meditation

The focus of this book is on creating sacred space and learning how to recognize, harness, and utilize energy to benefit your well-being. One of my goals is to inspire each of us to create a safe place to explore ways to awaken the divine energy that resides in us all. Once your sacred space has been created, the next logical step is to explore the path of meditation to personalize your journey of growth and awakening. This path of exploration will be unique to you.

Many people ask, "what's up" with meditation? What can it really do for me?" Meditation is way that anyone can use to help cope with stress, anxiety, and medical problems through thought, contemplation and reflection. Meditation encompasses a variety of practices that are somewhat different, but all of which share the basic principles of consideration and quiet thought. Buddhist, Chakra Taoist, Transcendental, Zen and prayer are just a few examples of various types of meditation. Some methods require stillness in the body, while others allow total freedom in movement. Regardless of the path that you choose, they all utilize contemplation and reflection to quiet the mind and free it from stress.

In this world of chaos and negativity, most of us are unaware of just how much stress we hold on to. When our bodies are exposed to a sudden threat we respond with hormones that are released from the adrenal glands as our pulse races, the blood pressure increases, our breath becomes faster and the blood rushes to our muscles. We have inherited this survival response from our ancestors. With the constant barrage of negative energy we encounter on a daily basis and our inability to control these situations, the same ancient response is triggered, but without the primal release of being able to act on the perceived "threat." As a result, we end up in a permanent loop of stress.

Meditation is a practice that brings about both and psychological benefits. Relaxation and decreased physical stress are the obvious benefits, but meditation can also improve moods, memory, decrease depression and have amazing effects on the psyche. A regular meditation practice, even for as little as ten minutes a day, will bring the following benefits:

- Reduced stress and tension
- Help in keeping blood pressure normal
- Enhanced energy, strength, and vigor
- Reduced anxiety, as it lowers the levels of blood lactate
- Increased self confidence
- Increased serotonin, which influences moods and behavior. (Low levels of serotonin are associated with depression.)
- Increased concentration and a strengthened mind
- A state of deep relaxation and general feeling of well-being

Four Basic Elements of Traditional Meditation

A Quiet Place

The best environment for the practice of meditation is a quiet place with minimum distractions, which will help you progressively relax your body's muscles.

A Comfortable Posture

The major characteristics of the prescribed meditation postures in many traditions are that the spine be kept straight. This is true in the traditions of the Hindu and Buddhist yogas, the Christian tradition of kneeling in prayer, and the Taoist standing meditation of "embracing the pillar."

In the beginning, people with misalignments may feel uncomfortable when assuming these postures. Over time the postures help put the spine back into a structurally sound line. The weight of the body gets distributed around the spine

in a balanced pattern and gravity, not muscular tension, takes over as the primary influence.

A sitting posture is better for meditation than lying down, which can easily lead to sleep. In traditional meditation postures, the back is kept erect, though not rigid. This is called a "poised posture" and it promotes the right state of attention-awareness for successful meditation.

An Object to Dwell On

In Hindu yoga, the object the attention dwells on is often a mantra, usually a Sanskrit word or syllable. In Buddhism the focus for the attention is the breath. Both mantra meditation and awareness of breathing fulfill the elements required for relaxing meditation.

Some meditation methods involve looking at objects with open eyes, while others the subjects close their eyes, which makes relaxation easier to induce. There is much to be said for choosing either a neutral word or meaningless sound from mantra meditation. Studies indicate that the brain wave patterns during meditation result in the deepest relaxation when thoughts are absent. Mantras are a good way to help focus the mind and eliminate conscious thought.

Poised Awareness and Passive Attitudes

Poised awareness is essential for relaxation and alertness to merge in perfect balance. If awareness of breathing is your single meditation method, you might let your attention dwell on the gentle rise of your abdomen. Your breathing will become very quiet after a few minutes of meditation. The rhythm and gentle movement of abdominal breathing will promote relaxation.

Passive attitudes happen when external distractions (from environmental sounds and intrusive thoughts and images) are viewed with detachment and are casually let go of. Each time you become aware that your attention has slipped away from your breathing or mantra and notice that you've start engaging in logical thinking, or you've begun paying attention to external sounds or other sensations, you will bring your focus back to your breathing, your mantra, or meditation object of choice. With practice, moments of great calm and deep relaxation during your meditation will become more frequent.

Meditation Postures

Depending on your flexibility there are many postures you can use in meditation. Listed below are a few poses to try in order of their difficulty: from the Egyptian, which is easiest, to the Burmese, the Za Zen and culminating with the Half Lotus.

The Egyptian

This is an easy posture for the beginner or for those who might have flexibility issues in sitting on the floor. Find a chair that allows you to sit upright. If necessary, put a pillow behind your back to attain a poised posture. Cup your hands in your lap with your thumbs touching and wrists at the top of your thighs.

The Burmese

In this simple posture the legs are not crossed but the knees are spread and stay down with the legs folded and the feet pulled back in front of the pelvis with one foot in front of the other. The cupped hands rest on the tops of the thighs or on the heels. It's important to have a firm cushion to sit on and a folded rug or blanket below to prevent pain to the feet and ankles. The buttocks should be pushed slightly out to bring the back into an easy upright posture.

The Za Zen

This classic meditation posture allows for easy extension of the spine. Place a Zafu pillow under the pelvis and kneel with legs on either side of the Zafu. Tilt pelvis slightly back extend the spine upward. Cup your hands in your lap with your thumbs touching and wrists at the top of your thighs.

The Half Lotus

The Half Lotus position has been used around the world for meditation and ceremony since the beginning of man and provides a comfortable sitting position for resting the mind during meditation. In a sitting position, stretch your legs straight out. Bend your left leg at the knee and bring it toward you and take hold of your left foot with both hands. Place your left foot so that the sole rests against the inside of the right thigh. The heel of your left foot should be drawn in as far as possible. Bend your right leg at the knee and take hold of your right foot with both hands. Place your right foot in the fold of your left leg. Drop the right knee as far as you can go toward the floor. Rest your hands on your knees. When your legs grow tired, stretch out and massage your knees and proceed to reverse positions of your legs starting with your right first.

Mantras for Meditation

Mantra meditation is a technique used to bring your physical, emotional, mental and spiritual body in tune with the universal vibration. Scientifically, sounds have been proven to have a profound impact on the body and brain, which is worth consideration and must be experienced to truly understand.

A mantra is a word or words you choose to repeat as you exhale during meditating. An example is: OM, which is symbolic of the universal energy that courses through all living matter. When saying the word (pronounced) ahh-ohh-mmm a vibration will be felt through your whole head and, as rumination deepens, your body as well.

Some other examples of Hindu mantras might be: sat nan (which represents truth); so hum, (which represents the paradox of life); or the Buddhist mantra om shanty shanty shanty om (meaning past, present and future); shanty (meaning peace) repeated three times is interpreted as threefold peace in body, speech and mind.

There are many mantras to explore and I recommend doing your own research to learn the meanings and origins of different mantras, and to see what resonates with you for your meditation practice.

Using Your Sacred Space

Mala Beads for Meditation

A mala is a string of beads used to count mantras (Sanskrit prayers) in sets of 108 repetitions. A mantra is a word or series of words chanted out loud or silently to invoke spiritual qualities. In the yogic tradition, a mantra is a Sanskrit word that has special powers to transform consciousness, promote healing or fulfill desires.

Some of my clients have asked what the significance is of 108 beads. I was taught that in some traditions that the number 1 stood for God, the 0 stood for completeness, and the 8 stood for eternity.

Mala beads are tools used to keep your mind on the meditation practice. Malas are often made of tulsi (basil wood), sandalwood, rosewood, rudraksh seeds or various healing stones and crystals. Each type of material has specific properties that can subtly affect the subconscious mind. Researching these properties will help guide you to decide which to use for your own meditation practice.

The mala is traditionally held in the right hand and can be used in two ways:

1. The mala hangs between the thumbs and the ring (third) finger. The middle (second) finger is used to rotate the mala by one bead towards oneself with each repetition of the mantra.

2. The mala hangs on the middle finger, and the thumb is used to rotate the mala one bead at a time.

Either way, the index finger is never touched.

The practice begins at the summit bead (sumeru) and continues around the loop until the summit is reached again. The summit bead is never passed over. If you plan to continue beyond the 108 repetitions, you would turn the mala around then repeat the process as long as you wish.

A mantra can be a gift from a teacher, or you can choose a mala for yourself. When selecting a mantra, be clear about your intention for your practice and use your intuition over your intellect to make your choice. You might want to try out each mantra for a few repetitions to see how it resonates with you and then choose the one that feels the best.

Using the Mala Beads in Meditation

Sit in a comfortable position, with eyes closed and repeat your mantra either silently or aloud, moving through the beads in a loop from summit to summit. Focus your mind on your mantra, let go of conscious thoughts, and make your breath slow and deep.

To empower the mala and your mantra, Japa (mantra meditation) should be practiced each day for 40 continuous days. When the mala becomes empowered, it can be worn or lightly placed on oneself or others to transmit the energy of the mantra as well as the energetic qualities of the mala itself.

When you use a new mantra with a mala, this energy becomes replaced, so it is advised that you use a new mala with each new mantra if possible. When not in use, be sure to store your mala in a special clean space; preferably on your personal altar or statue of a deity.

Altared Space | 57

Using Your Sacred Space

Chakras

The word chakra comes from the Sanskrit word that means wheel. There are seven major chakras beginning at the base of the spine and finishing at the top of the head. Although they are fixed in the central spine, they are located on both the front and back of the body and work through it.

Each chakra vibrates and rotates at different speeds: The root or first chakra moves at the slowest speed and the crown, or the seventh chakra moves the fastest.

Each of the chakras is stimulated by its complementary color and a variety of gemstones used for specific healing power.

The size and brightness of the wheels vary with individual development, physical condition, energy levels, stress, or disease.

When the chakras are not balanced, or if the energy is blocked, you may feel tired, out of sorts, or depressed and your basic life force will be slowed down. Any fear, doubt or negativity that may preoccupy you can affect bodily functions and lead to disease.

Actively creating a constant balance among the chakras is vital to your physical, mental health and well-being.

When we block our feelings to unpleasant experiences it interrupts the energy flow. This effects the natural development and maturation of the chakra's growth, often leaving the chakra disfigured. When the chakras are functioning in balance, they will be open and spinning to metabolize the particular energies needed from the universal energy field.

Root, The First Chakra

The root chakra is located at the base of the spine at the tailbone in back and the pubic bone in the front of the body. This center holds the basic needs for survival, security, and safety. It is powerfully connected to Mother Earth, providing us with the ability to stay grounded to the earth plane. This is the center for manifestation. When you are trying to make things happen in the material business world or for material possessions, the energy to succeed will come from this energy center. If this chakra is blocked, you may feel anxious insecure, fearful and frustrated. Problems like obesity, anorexia, and knee troubles may occur. Root body parts include the hips, legs, lower back, and sexual organs.

A man's sexual organs are located in his first chakra and his sexual energy is usually experienced as physical. Woman's sexual organs are located in the second chakra and usually experienced as emotion. Both chakras are associated with sexual energy.

Healing Associations

ELEMENT: Earth
MUSICAL NOTE: C
PLANT: Sage
COLORS: Red, Brown, Black

GEMSTONES: Ruby Hematite, Bloodstone, Garnet, Smoky Quartz, Obsidian, and Black Tourmaline
ESSENTIAL OILS: Patchouli, Cedarwood, and Vetivar
GOVERNS: stability, patience, security, structure, the ability to manifest your dreams
REMEDIES: Movement of any kind that activates the feet and legs, connecting with nature enjoying its natural beauty. Any form of physical activity that requires presence. Perseverance, finding trust in place of despair, to find value in the material as sacred.

Sacral, The Second Chakra

The second chakra is referred to as the belly or sacral. It's located two inches below the navel and is rooted into the spine. This center holds the basic needs for sexuality, creativity, intuition, self worth, friendliness, and emotions. It governs one's sense of self worth, confidence in one's creativity and the ability to relate to others in an open and friendly way. It is governed by how emotions were either repressed or expressed in the family dynamic during childhood. When in balance, this chakra allows emotions to flow freely, and allows one to feel and reach out to others (sexually or not).

When this chakra is blocked, a person may feel emotionally explosive, manipulative, obsessed with thoughts of sex or a complete lack of energy. Physical problems can include constipation, stiff lower back, weak kidneys, and muscle spasms. Belly body parts include the sexual organs (women), kidneys, bladder, and large intestine.

Healing Associations

ELEMENT: Water
MUSICAL NOTE: D
PLANT: Jasmine
COLOR: Orange

GEMSTONES: Tigers Eye, Carnelian, Onyx, Orange Calcite
ESSENTIAL OILS: Spruce, Jasmine, Orange blossom, Myrtle, Clary Sage
GOVERNS: Sexuality, Pleasure, Well being and Abundance
REMEDIES: Yoga , Meditation Dancing, Fasting, Swimming, not linking your self worth with what you have or do, create healthy boundaries to protect your vital force.

Solar Plexus, The Third Chakra

The third chakra is the solar plexus, located two inches below the breastbone in the center behind the stomach. This is the center of personal power, ego, passions, impulses, strength, and anger. It is also the center of astral travel and astral influences, psychic development and receptivity of spirit guides. When the solar plexus is in balance you have self-respect, enjoy taking on new challenges, have a strong sense of personal power, and you feel cheerful, outgoing, and expressive.

When out of balance, the third chakra will exhibit confusion, lack of confidence, depression, worries about what other people think, or allowing others to take control of your life. Physical problems may include digestive difficulties, liver problems, diabetes, nervous exhaustion and food allergies. The body parts for the third chakra include the stomach, liver, gall bladder, pancreas, and small intestine.

Healing Associations

ELEMENT: Fire
MUSICAL NOTE: E
PLANT: Carnation
COLOR: Yellow
GEMSTONES: Amber, Citrine, Yellow Calcite, Topaz
ESSENTIAL OILS: Lemon, Lemongrass, Grapefruit, Ginger & Juniper
GOVERNS: Personal Power, Self Worth, Confidence, Self Esteem
REMEDIES: Develop a strong resilient ego, competitive sports hiking, cycling, taking leadership positions, acting-amateur theater

Using Your Sacred Space

Heart, the Fourth Chakra

The fourth chakra is the Heart Chakra and is located behind the breast bone in front of the spine and between the shoulder blades. This is the center for love, compassion and spirituality. This center directs ones abilities to love oneself and to give and receive love. The Heart Chakra also connects the body and mind with spirit. When in balance, this chakra resonates with compassion, the desire to nurture, and to see the good in everyone.

Almost everyone has suffered from a broken heart. Deep heart hurts can result in aura obstructions called heart scars. When these heart scars are released, they raise a lot of old pain, but free the heart for healing and new growth. When the fourth chakra is out of balance, being afraid of getting hurt, letting go, or feeling unworthy of love comes to play, leaving you with a sense of paranoia, feeling sorry for your self and being indecisive. Physical illnesses include high blood pressure, insomnia, difficulty in breathing and heart attack. Body parts for the fourth chakra include the heart, lungs, circulatory system, shoulders, and upper back.

Healing Associations

ELEMENT: Air
MUSICAL NOTE: F
PLANT: Rose, Foxglove, Lily
COLORS: Green (for the heart protector) Pink or Gold (for the heart itself)
GEMSTONES: Rose Quartz, Kunzite, Diamond, Peridot, Watermelon Tourmaline
ESSENTIAL OILS: Rose, Cardamon Bergamot, & Geranium
REMEDIES: Massage, Yoga, Walking, Prayer, letting love be the center of your life starting with loving yourself first then others, any joyful endeavor such as singing or dancing.

Using Your Sacred Space

Throat, The Fifth Chakra

The fifth chakra is the Throat Chakra. This chakra is located in the "V" of the collar bone at the lower back and is the center of communication, sound, expression of creativity via thought, speech and writing. The possibility of change, transformation and healing are here. When in balance you may feel centered, inspired either musically or artistically and you may be a good speaker.

When this chakra is out of balance, you may feel weak, want to hold back, feel timid, be quiet or have a hard time communicating your thoughts. Physical illnesses may include sore throats, hyperthyroid, inflammations, back pain, and skin irritation.

Healing Associations

ELEMENT: The Ethers in which all things are contained
MUSICAL NOTE: G
PLANT: Gardenia
COLORS: Turquoise, Light Blue
GEMSTONES: Aquamarine, Blue Agate, Azurite, Turquoise
ESSENTIAL OILS: Eucalyptus, Gardenia, Ylang Ylang, Blue Chamomile, Lavender, and Holy Basil

REMEDIES: Expressing your highest truth, to live creatively with integrity. Yoga, Tai Chi, Cranio-Sacral Therapy, Dance, Meditation, Chanting, Singing, Keeping a Journal, Public Speaking

Third Eye, The Sixth Chakra

The Sixth Chakra is the third eye. It is located above the physical eyes on the center of the forehead. This is the center for psychic ability, higher intuition, the energies of spirit, and light. The third eye assists in the purification of the negative tendencies and the elimination of selfish attitudes. With the power of the Sixth Chakra, you are able to receive guidance, channel and tune into your higher self. When in balance, the third eye opens you to being your own master with no fear of death, with no attachment to material things. You may experience telepathy, astral travel, and past lives.

When the Sixth Chakra is out of balance you may be afraid of success, nonassertive, or the complete opposite, egotistical. Physical symptoms may include eyestrain, headaches, blurred vision and blindness. The Sixth Chakra body parts include the brain, eyes, face, lymphatic system and endocrine systems.

Healing Associations

ELEMENTS: The Cosmos
MUSICAL NOTE: A
PLANT: Almond Blossom
COLORS: Indigo, Purple
GEMSTONES: Amethyst, Lapis, Lazuli, Sapphire, Sodalite, Tanzinite
ESSENTIAL OILS: Sandalwood, Champa, and Spikenard
REMEDIES:, Discerning what your highest and greatest joy might be, trusting your intuition, Contemplation, Meditation, Creative Visualization, Tai chi, Yoga

Crown, The Seventh Chakra

The Seventh Chakra is the Crown Chakra. It is located just behind the top of the skull. It is the center of spirituality, enlightenment, dynamic thought and energy. It brings the gift of cosmic consciousness, allowing for the inward flow of wisdom. This is the center of connectedness with the divine, the place where all life animates the physical body. The Crown is where the soul comes into the body and exists upon death. When the Crown is in balance we have total access to the sub-conscious and unconscious, allowing us to open up to the divine.

When out of balance, we may experience frustration, along with destructive feelings and a lack of joy in our lives. Depression and migraine headaches may occur when this chakra is misaligned.

Healing Associations

ELEMENT: The Cosmos
MUSICAL NOTE: B
PLANT: Lotus Flower
COLOR: Violet
GEMSTONES: Alexandrite, Amethyst, Clear Quartz, Oregon Opal
ESSENTIAL OILS: Frankincense, Myrrh, Ceadarwood Angelica, and Neroli

REMEDIES: Reflection, Stillness, Meditation, Prayer. To create a resilient spiritual context through self realization of your souls purpose and your connection with the greater good that is within all of us.

Healing Therapies
74 | Altared Space

Healing Therapies

Healing with Crystals

Crystal therapy or healing is a form of vibrational medicine. Gemstones house spiritual and healing properties that can be tapped into a variety of ways. Crystals can be worn by the individual or placed in a location where they can emit their healing vibrations and be felt by whoever is nearby. They can be placed on a reclined individual to balance the chakras during a healing session. One of the bet reference books on crystals I have found is *The Book Of Stones,* which I highly recommend to further your knowledge on the properties of crystals, chakra correspondence, and which stones work best together to benefit your healing process.

Clearing is necessary before using any stone for healing. The clearer the energy of a healing stone the more powerful the healing.

The first and most traditional way to clear a stone is the use of sea salt. The sea salt can either be dissolved in water or used dry. It is considered one of the most powerful ways to disperse of any dis-ease or negativity left in the stone. Be sure to use sea salt as table salt contains aluminum and other chemicals.

Regardless whether you choose wet or dry immersion, do not use plastic or metal containers. If you are immersing in water, use a glass or ceramic container with cold water and a tablespoon of salt. In dry salt immersion, you should bury the stones in the salt with points pointing downwards. For both methods leave the stones overnight. Do not place your stones in direct sunlight as some of the stones are susceptible to fading and internal fractures could cause your stones to crack or break.

Other cleansing methods include: giving your crystals a "moon bath" from the full to the new moon or burying your crystals in the earth, which is especially helpful when you feel a deep cleansing is needed. Another method would be to bury your stones in a cupful of herbs such as rose petals, sage, frankincense, myrrh, and sandalwood. This is a gentle way to clear, however it may take a longer than the sea salt method.

Healing Therapies
78 | Altared Space

Healing with Essential Oils

Man has used herbs for healing since the beginning of human history. The "Rig Veda" written more than 5,000 years ago talks of the healing powers of herbs. The ancient ayurvedic texts describe a fairly sophisticated method used to concentrate the aromas. At some point in time the extraction method was perfected through the process of steam distillation.

Today, potent aromatic plant substances gained through a steam distillation process are available to improve your health and mental well-being. These are called essential oils. They contain the most subtle, ethereal and volatile aspects of the plant.

At the beginning of the 20th century, French chemist Maurice Gattefosse analyzed the chemical composition of essential oils and wrote the first book on their pharmacology, which he called "aromatherapy." Since that time, numerous studies have confirmed the healing properties of essential oils. The direct neural influence of the sense of smell on the limbic system makes aromatherapy an ideal tool to improve the emotional and other stress-related imbalances in the individual.

In the pages dedicated to the chakras, I included a list of healing tools and associations for use in meditation at the altar. Included are the essential oils that directly relate to stimulating and healing the individual chakras. One of my mentors, Allison Stillman, has written a book called *The Sacred Art of Anointing*, which is a good read for those interested in learning both the history and current knowledge on the sacred art of healing with essential oils. (See Resources" for further information on Allison's work.)

Healing Therapies
80 | Altared Space

Healing with Sound

For centuries, healers have intuitively used the therapeutic powers of sound. Many tools have been used to aid healing and to create music: planetary gongs, Tibetan bowls, didgeridoos, rattles and drums to name a few. Today, practitioners are rediscovering sound as a tool for realignment and healing the body. Utilizing modern methods, healers are also using tuning forks, chimes, sound discs, and resonator plates in their practice.

Sound is produced when an object is vibrating in a random or periodic repeated motion. Every object has a frequency-vibration that creates sound. All matter, when broken down into subatomic particles, consists of pulsating (vibrating) energy fields. This includes the human body in all of its facets, from physical, emotional, and spiritual: the body gives off and is affected by frequency vibration.

In our modern world, most of our bodies have lost connection to the power and magic of the inner world and great cycles of the universe that inform it. Sound can move into form, take shape and help us reconnect with this inner world. People have reported a variety of sensations during sound treatments that include seeing various lighted shapes, colors, geometric shapes and other visions. Modern science has shown that our auditory nerves are linked to our sense of proportion and balance, and they have the power to shift our energy to the center, bringing about a feeling of connection and serenity.

In many cultures, healers and shamans have understood that listening to vibrational sound helps us access these auditory nerves in a way that increases our receptivity to healing energy. Great musicians of our times have known and written about the transcendent power of sound that can bring a listener to a divine state. The sounds used in a healing session induce a shift in consciousness that helps the person to get unstuck in their beliefs about misfortune and disease. Specifically, it is the no-tone or silence in between tones that takes the person back to their pure state of being and has the healing effect.

In the following pages, I will introduce you to some common methods of healing with sound that you may choose to explore.

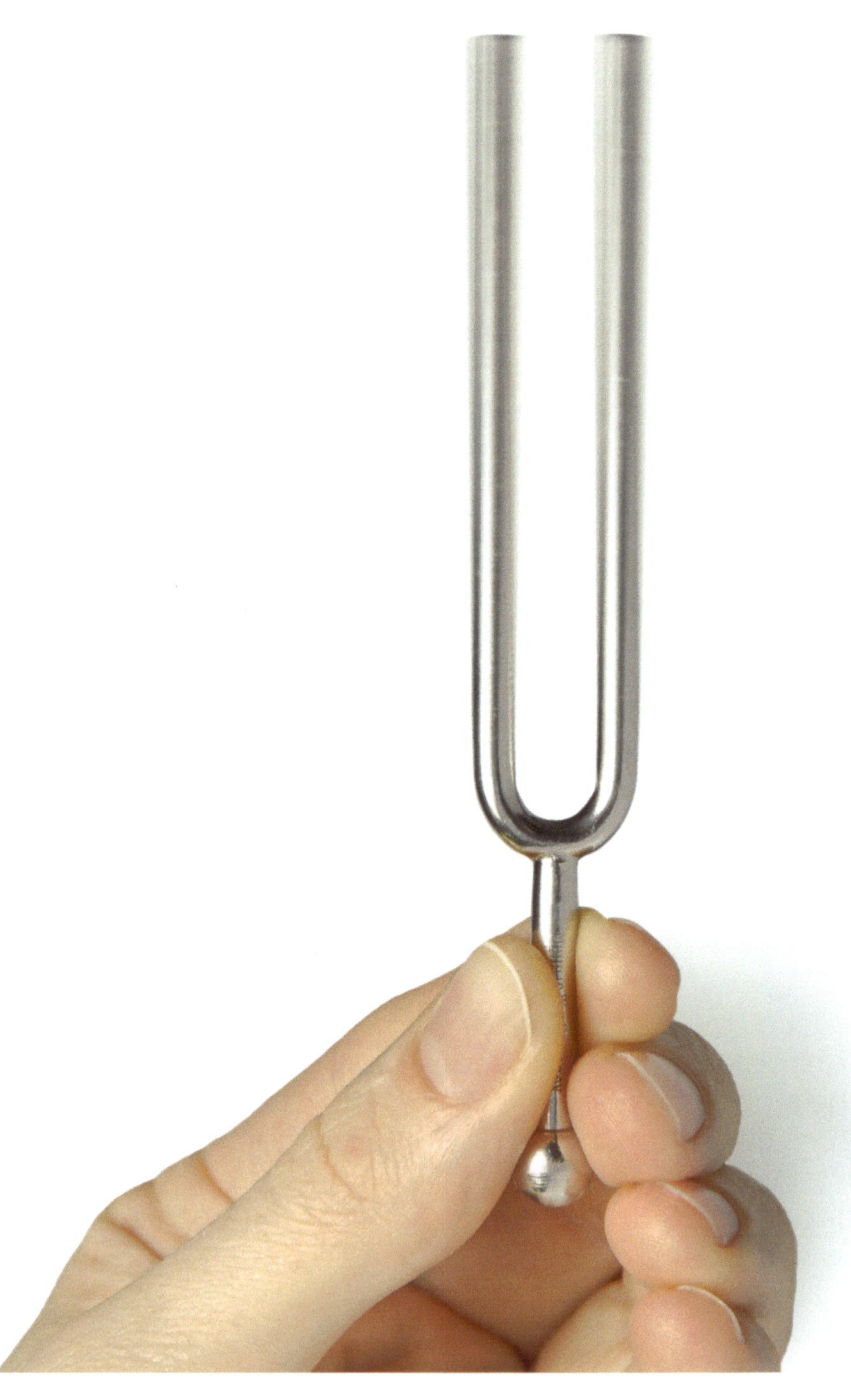

Healing Therapies

Tuning Fork Sound Therapy

The human body is sustained by life force energy, which is referred to as "chi" in Chinese or "prana" in Indian medicine. This energy, which has electro-magnetic characteristics, travels through your body's chakras to nurture all the main organs, glands, muscles, nerves, tissue, and cells.

Sound is in constant motion and is made up of three important interconnecting elements: pulse, wave, and form. When the human body comes in contact with these sound elements, either a negative or positive resonance occurs and the body's delicate cell structure is affected. Resonance is the process where the primary vibration initiates a secondary vibration, which becomes sympathetic to the first, and they both start resonating at the same frequency.

In tuning fork therapy, a beneficial process of resonance occurs. Focusing the vibrations of sound generated by tuning forks on various parts of the body can help establish a new pattern of balance, erasing the detrimental patterns caused by the negative resonance of ill health.

Tuning forks are made of special aluminum alloy, which gives the sounds generated a rich overtone of warmth and depth. They have a long ringing decay time, so that the note is sustained as long as possible. The tuning fork can be administered in a very focused point to specific parts of the body that are suffering from pain and discomfort. Tuning forks may also be focused or spiraled into the chakra vortices and nerve plexus positions, or they may be waved over the body in a figure eight pattern to give a sound bath to the aura.

Tuning fork sound therapy can help alleviate many health problems, from pain control to emotional and behavioral problems. Using tuning forks often has a soothing effect on the nervous system and is good for tension-related illness caused by stress. The relaxation and new-found energy this therapy can bring to an individual often results in profound changes by unblocking the chakra, causing it to reboot its own innate healing energy where it is needed most.

Healing Therapies

Singing Bowls

Traditional Singing Bowls

Singing bowls (also know as Tibetan, Himalayan or medicine bowls, rin gongs, and suzu gongs) are classified as a standing bell with the bottom surface resting and the sides and rim vibrating to produce sound. Traditionally, they were used throughout Asia in spiritual practice. Today they are employed worldwide within and without of spiritual traditions, for meditation, relaxation, trance-induction, healthcare, personal well-being and religious practice.

Singing bowls are played by applying friction with a wooden or leather-wrapped mallet around the rim of the bowl to produce overtones and a continuous singing sound. High quality singing bowls produce a complex chord of harmonic overtones and may also be played by striking the rim with soft mallet to produce a warm bell tone.

Singing bells are unique in that they are multi-phonic instruments, producing multiple harmonic overtones at the same time. Alloys made with multiple metals are used to create the bowls. The specific alloys used produce the specific kinds of overtones in the bowls.

Traditional manufacturing techniques have been largely lost, however, there are new bowls being produced with old hand-hammered methods. The difference in today's bowls versus ancient bowls is in the quality of the alloy and the aging process itself. The tone improves as they age so the new bowls will not sound as warm and mellow as a real antique.

The allow mix for antique bowls often included silver, gold, nickel and the most prized "sky iron" from meteorites, which produced multi-phonic and poly-harmonic overtones, making them highly prized for their tonal qualities. New singing bowls are also made of bronze alloy, however they usually does not include gold and silver. The best handmade examples now come from Nepal, followed by Japan and Korea. Both new and antique bowls are used in meditation practice, yoga, sound healing, music therapy religious services and personal enjoyment.

Healing Therapies
86 | Altared Space

Crystal Singing Bowls

Crystal singing bowls are made from pure quartz silica sand, which is poured into a centrifugal spinning mold. A torch is then applied, the sand is heated to thousands of degrees, and the particles integrate to become amorphous, making the transition from crystalline to a glassy structure. The bowls are then shaped to resonate at different tones. Quartz oscillates at a very high frequency. It amplifies and transmits energy and is used on computer motherboards, watches, and many other technologies. Quartz has memory and can be programmed with intent, which makes them it very powerful tool when used in meditation and healing work.

Crystal singing bowls emit a very high sine (pure tone) wave that carries through a form very readily. Our bodies have a natural affinity to quartz and are composed of many crystalline substances. Our bones, blood, and DNA are crystalline. Our brains also have a liquid crystal-colloidal structure. Even on a molecular level, our cells contain silica, which balances our electromagnetic energies. This is the same formula as natural quartz crystal. The rich resonance of the crystal bowls causes the crystalline structures within our bodies to vibrate and resonate, resulting in a profound response. The various tones affect our chakras as they open, balance and heal.

Vibrations from a crystal singing bowl can awaken cellular memories and hold the vibration of pure white light, which contains the full color spectrum when refracted. Playing the bowls infuses us with sound and light, and fills our auras with vibrational radiance that embodies the seven main colors of the rainbow.

As different parts of the brain are affected, they release different hormones and neuro chemicals that can suppress pain, strengthen willpower, enhance creativity and overcome addictions.

Crystal singing bowl vibrations have the power to shift our consciousness in a positive way. The rich tones evoked affect brain activity, which facilitates altered states of consciousness. As our awareness expands, we grow closer to our original selves and begin to reflect our highest good while still in our physical form.

Healing Therapies

Gong Sound Therapy

Gongs have been used since prehistoric times and are found all over the world. While there are many types of gongs, the kind used most often in mediation is a flat, circular disc of metal suspended vertically by cords from a standing frame.

A skilled musician or devotee can create a wide range of sounds from a gong that can have amazing effects on the listener's state of mind. During reflection, the mind can enter a state where it is very open to thought and consideration. While in that state, the sound from the gong can penetrate and support your intentions and create a tangible, physical resonance that vibrates throughout the whole body, leading to a unique experience of altered consciousness.

The sound of the gong also resonates through all of the chakras and can be used as a powerful instrument to open and balance them. Certain areas of the gong resonate with different chakra centers, opening and balancing these centers, and causing the cells of the body to move and release blockages.

Nothing compares with the gong's ability to create sounds that bring us to a state of harmony. It takes only 3-90 seconds for the gong to have an effect on the mind. As the gong is played, it produces a note against the background of another, thereby creating a complex pattern of sounds that you feel in your body. The sound waves help open the subconscious mind to a deep meditative state, giving us the opportunity to expand our own psyche to new aspects of ourselves.

Aside from actually learning to play your own personal gong, there are other ways to engage in gong meditation. One way would be to purchase a CD. You can also find a local gong meditation group, which may be the best way to physically experience altered states of consciousness while in a relaxed meditative state. Before starting your gong journey, I would highly recommend a book called *Gong Yoga* to learn more about the origin, history and use of gongs for yoga, meditation and current applications for healing and transformation. (See resources for more information)

IN CLOSING

I would like thank all of my mentors, clients, friends, and loved ones who encouraged me to take on this project. I hope this book clearly presents the information and provides the inspiration to take your own journey at the Altar for the peace and serenity that you certainly deserve. On the preceding pages I've listed mentors who have taught me well and, just in case you found yourself resonating to a particular subject matter found on these pages, I also listed a few books I feel would help further your knowledge.

    Namaste~ Nicholas Cappele

Nicholas Cappele, founder and principle of H2E Design, has been in the interior design business for over 30 years. His work has been nationally recognized in *Sources and Design*, *Phoenix Home & Garden*, the *Arizona Republic* and *Prescott Woman Magazine*.

Nicholas's lifelong practice of Feng Shui, meditation and yoga inspired him to write this first book, *Altared Space: Harnessing Healing Energy Using Feng Shui Principles*, which focuses on how to create sacred space for meditation using these principles for health and well-being.

Along with his design practice, Nicholas conducts interactive workshops teaching basic Feng Shui principles for creating sacred spaces. The main objective of these workshops is to develop awareness and understanding of connectivity and energy flow as a key to a balanced life of health and prosperity.

When Nicholas decided to create his furniture line, his mission was to engage and support local artists and be as green as possible by using non-endangered materials that can be recycled well. In addition, his Feng Shui, meditation and yoga practices inspired him to research and develop his line of essential oil blends, soy-based candles and bath products specifically devoted to healing the body and mind through the use of natural plant essences.

Learn more about Nicholas, H2E Design, his workshops and product lines at www.h2edesignstore.com.

MENTOR AKNOWLEDGEMENTS AND RESOURCES

DENISE LIOTTA-DENNIS www.drangongatefengshui.net	My classic Feng Shui master, many thanks for enlightening me to the ancient ways of the Chinese Masters.
NATHALIE EKOBO www.bemagnifque.com	My intuitive business coach, many thanks for inspiration and encouragement to follow my dreams.
PAMELA DONISON www.donisonlaw.com	Attorney, mediator, peacemaker, client and mentor, many thanks for your encouragement to "put it writing"!
MARY BETH MARKUS www.desertsongyoga.com	Owner/ yoga master of Desert Song yoga studio in Phoenix AZ, many thanks to you and your expert staff for teaching me the Anusara principles in keeping balance in life & finding my inner peace.
ALLISON STILLMAN www.romancingthedivine.com	My essential oil guru, many thanks to opening my mind to the amazing healing powers of plant essence.
JILL BERNSTEIN jillbcreative@gmail.com	Many thanks to your brilliant insight in creating "flow" to this material with your editing skills

BOOKS TO INSPIRE YOUR ALTARED JOURNEY

The Essence of the Bhagavad Gita
Parhamhansa Yogananda
The Book of Stones
Robert Simmons and Naisha Ahsian
The Sacred Art of Anointing
Allison Stillman
Gong Yoga
Methab Benton
Building Wealth with Feng Shui
Denise – Liotta Dennis
The Monk Who Sold His Ferrari
Robin S. Sharma

CONTRIBUTING PHOTOGRAPHERS

Lani Conklin
www.blackmoonimages.com
Dave Davis
www.davedavisphotography.com
Ken Hester
hester0527@msn.com
Nicholas Cappele
www.h2einteriors.com
Lydia Von-anhalt

FEATURED ARTISTS

Robert Miley pg 34, 58
Laura Plecas pg 41, 57
Hunter (Phx art Group) pg 32
John Douglas (Phx Art Group) pg 40

www.ingramcontent.com/pod-product-compliance
Lightning Source LLC
Chambersburg PA
CBHW042022150426
43198CB00002B/42